SHUTTING DOWN BULLIES

SHUTTING DOWN
VIOLENT BULLIES

Pam T. Glaser and Alexandra Hanson-Harding

rosen publishing's
rosen
central

New York

Published in 2020 by The Rosen Publishing Group, Inc.
29 East 21st Street, New York, NY 10010

Copyright © 2020 by The Rosen Publishing Group, Inc.

First Edition

Library of Congress Cataloging-in-Publication Data

Names: Glaser, Pam T., author. | Hanson-Harding, Alexandra, author.
Title: Shutting down violent bullies / Pam T. Glaser and Alexandra Hanson-Harding.
Description: First edition. | New York : Rosen Publishing, 2020. | Series:
Shutting down bullies | Includes bibliographical references and index.
Identifiers: LCCN 2019013390| ISBN 9781725347014 (library bound) | ISBN 9781725347007 (pbk.)
Subjects: LCSH: Bullying—Prevention—Juvenile literature.
Classification: LCC BF637.B85 G534 2020 | DDC 302.34/3—dc23
LC record available at https://lccn.loc.gov/2019013390

Manufactured in the United States of America

Some of the images in this book illustrate individuals who are models.
The depictions do not imply actual situations or events.

CONTENTS

Introduction

In 2017, a middle schooler from Tennessee named Keaton Jones shared a video he had made with his mom's help. In it, he asked, "Why do they bully?" and talked about some of his experiences at school with bullies making fun of his appearance or hurting him physically. He concluded by saying, "It'll probably get better one day." The video went viral, and lots of people on Twitter shared their own stories of being bullied when they were Keaton's age. Celebrities began to weigh in as well. Demi Lovato said, "There are so many people who come out of bullying so much stronger and you will be one of them!!" Cardi B went a step further, offering advice to parents: "Please teach your kids not to be bullies." Actor Chris Evans offered Keaton a chance to attend an Avengers movie premiere with him. Anyone can be the victim of a bully: adults and kids, of any gender.

But how do you recognize when actions cross the line from roughhousing or messing around into bullying? "Bullying

Actor Chris Evans, best known for his role as Captain America in the *Avengers* films, offered support to Keaton Jones.

4

is when someone is being hurt either by words or actions on purpose, usually more than once, feels bad because of it, and has a hard time stopping what is happening to them," according to the PACER Center's Kids Against Bullying website.

Bullying happens in a number of ways. One type is limited to verbal abuse, in which a bully calls someone names or makes other insulting remarks. Bullying can also be a passive act, in which the bully works to isolate a victim from friends or allies, sharing personal information or starting a rumor, without doing anything directly to hurt the person. There is bullying that takes place through social media or online. Probably the most widely understood type of bullying is physical or violent bullying, in which a bully hurts a person physically. This can include stealing or breaking someone's belongings or trapping him or her somewhere without the ability to escape.

Between one in four and one in three students in the United States says he or she has been bullied in school, according to StopBullying.gov. So what can you do if you're the victim of a bully, know someone who has been bullied, or are yourself a bully? Let's take a closer look at why bullies exist and what a young person can do to escape a violent bully.

The Targets of Violent Bullying

Teen antibullying advocate Jacob Law shared his own story of dealing with bullying in 2019. "I was pulled out [of my seat on the bus], thrown on the floor, and laughed at." Later, after attending a bullying prevention seminar at school, he realized that this wasn't just horseplay, but bullying. When Jacob tried to talk to a teacher about what was happening to him, he got reprimanded for leaving his seat during class. The teacher acted annoyed that she was being bothered. Jacob started faking being sick so he could miss school. The problems escalated when he started middle school, with students hitting him with spitballs, kicking him, trying to stuff him into a locker, or worse. When Jacob was a sophomore, later on in high school, he stayed up one night to start writing a suicide note to his parents. The next day at school, a girl noticed how tired he looked and asked him if he was okay. This act of caring started Jacob on a path not only toward escaping his own bullies, but also helping other young people escape theirs as well.

Jacob found the support he needed, but sometimes it's not so easy for victims of bullying. Many times, people who are

Spaces with limited supervision, like school buses, are often rife with physical bullying and other types of abuse because drivers can only do so much to help while operating a vehicle.

targets are unwilling to speak out. Even when they do, they don't feel truly heard—not by their parents, their teachers, or their school administrators.

Violent physical bullying can give targets stomachaches and headaches. It can make them lose their appetites. They can lose their concentration and their ability to sleep. It can make them withdraw and become isolated. Some students even avoid school altogether. Rates of depression typically skyrocket among bullying victims.

PROTECTING STUDENTS WITH SPECIAL NEEDS FROM BULLIES

Young people who have special needs in school are at a higher risk of being victimized by bullies. This includes physical or intellectual disabilities, learning or behavioral disorders, or illnesses or allergies that require special medical considerations in school environments. Students with disabilities are two to three times more likely to be bullied than nondisabled students, according to the National Bullying Prevention Center. There are ways to help, though! Creating an inclusive environment that includes lots of team activities can help a classroom become a more positive place for students with special needs. Often, young people don't know how to talk to or interact with people who are different, so learning about a peer's needs can help. Read up on autism, diabetes, food allergies, and epilepsy! Students with special needs and their families are encouraged to work with school officials to help make a classroom environment as welcoming and supportive as possible for a newcomer.

But as bad as those side effects are, the effects of physical bullying can be even worse. It can put students in severe danger.

Sometimes physical bullying causes victims to harm themselves. Nine-year-old McKenzie Adams of Demopolis, Alabama, was the victim of racist bullies who were angry at her for being friends with a white student (McKenzie was African American). McKenzie reported the bullying to teachers and the vice principal at her school, but nothing happened to fix the issue. In December 2018, she committed suicide.

WHAT MAKES A VICTIM?

Young people get bullied because a bully has made the decision not to respect the rights of others. However, there are reasons why some people are more likely than other people to become the target of a bully. Some of these reasons may seem fairly random.

Victims might be newcomers to a school, have an individual style of dress, or unusual interests. They might be extra tall or short, very thin or fat. Or they might be of a different ethnic group than the person who is bullying them. A child who is one of the few African Americans at his or her mostly white high school might be singled out as different by classmates and beaten by bullies. Many LGBTQ teens face bullying—often starting with name-calling and escalating to physical attacks.

JEALOUSY AND BULLYING

But people are also bullied for other reasons. Jealousy can be a factor. A bully might feel jealous of a smarter student who gets better grades or gets along better with teachers. Students driven by particular interests, like

Style of dress related to religious beliefs can often make a student a target.

drama club or another social or creative organization, might have a loyal circle of friends with similar interests. This can make a bully feel like an outsider and therefore want to destroy that social circle.

Some bullying victims are especially vulnerable because of their personalities. They may be people who are either naturally gentle or shy. They might be highly sensitive. These qualities are all positive in many ways. But they can make standing up to an aggressive bully more difficult.

THE PSYCHOLOGY OF VICTIMHOOD

Once bullying starts, the problem can increase quickly. One problem is that targets can start to believe that the bullying is their fault. The victim role becomes part of their identities. They might think, "I am being beaten because this is who I am." Instead they could think, "I am being beaten because this is something the bully did." Psychologists call this kind of thinking a victim schema.

When students feel threatened all the time, they tend to lose their sense of self-worth. They stop taking good care of themselves. They can also feel more hostile toward other students. They might be afraid. Bullies' targets may stop being able to recognize a neutral or even sympathetic face. Instead they might see enemies everywhere. The constant threat of danger makes it harder for these students to control their emotions. They can show behavior like anger, crying, or submissiveness at the wrong times. That behavior can push potential friends away. It rewards the bullies' desire to cause pain.

Victims of bullies often feel very alone and isolated. These feelings can lead to bouts of anxiety, depression, and even PTSD in certain cases.

PUTTING A STOP TO IT

No matter what symptoms victims show, no one deserves the injustice that is bullying. Everyone—including bystanders and especially the adults who are in charge of schools—needs to step in to keep bullying from intensifying. Being bullied is not a normal part of childhood, many experts now believe. They are concerned that it's a public health problem that needs to be taken seriously.

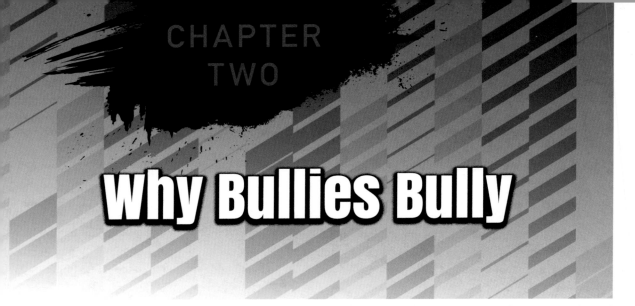

CHAPTER TWO

Why Bullies Bully

Sometimes, people ask those who are bullied, "What did you do to deserve this?" The assumption is that a victim makes himself or herself a target by being different or asking for it in some way. But the bigger question is: what makes bullies think they have the right to physically attack other people? Sadly, the answer is because they can. Unlike some other kinds of

Singer Taylor Swift has talked openly about her time as a teen dealing with bullying.

bullies, physical bullies are more likely to be male. They tend to be stronger and bigger than their targets and have undeservedly high self-esteem. Male bullies are usually among the oldest of their peer group, according to researcher Dan Olweus.

Psychology professor and expert on adolescent bullying Jaana Juvonen conducted a study on bullying by surveying two thousand children in Los Angeles, California. According to Dr. Juvonen, bullies tend to become popular early in middle school and act out as they try to adjust to the uncertainty of the new environment. This breeds a sense of dominance and this leads to bullying. Most studies show that bullies are usually people who either have a very high opinion of themselves or who are eager to maintain their popularity by any means possible. And bullying others can be an effective way for them to stay popular. For example, in her study, Juvonen and a colleague did an analysis of other studies and concluded that aggressive teens are actually more popular in high school than aggressive elementary students.

A recent study led by Robert Faris, a sociologist at the University of California, Davis, shows the complicated network of relationships between nearly four thousand eighth- through tenth-grade students over the course of a school year. This study, published by the *American Sociological Review*, found that teens' tendency toward aggressive behavior became greater the higher their social status rose—except for the very top 2 percent of students. "By and large, status increases aggression," said Faris. In many cases, the problem of bullying is compounded by the social power of many bullies' popularity.

According to Barbara Coloroso, author of the book *The Bully, the Bullied and the Bystander*, "Bullying is not about anger or conflict. It's about contempt—a powerful feeling of dislike toward someone considered to be worthless." She adds, "Once kids believe that someone is 'less than them,' they can harm that child without feeling any empathy, compassion or shame."

DIRTY FIGHTERS

The most important thing to remember about physical bullies is that they don't fight fair.

Physical bullies often pick unsupervised places around the school to attack their targets. Some examples are hallways, bathrooms, and on school buses. Other places include stairwells, paths on the way to school, and gyms. It's easier to get away with bullying if no one sees it happen.

Sometimes a group of bullies swarm a victim to hurt him or her. Other bullies attack their targets by surprise, shoving them

Bullying can even occur among sports teammates, a group that relies on camaraderie and teammwork in order to play well together.

BULLIES IN ADULTHOOD

Bullying can have long-term effects for those who are bullies as children and teens, including missing out on jobs and other opportunities. In a 2017 post of the "Ask a Manager" advice column, a highly qualified job seeker struggled to get an interview for a job in her field because, as a teen, she had bullied a girl who went on to work at the company with the job opening. "When I asked why, I was told a staffer had raised some concerns and the company would not be moving forward with my candidacy," the poster said in her letter.

Many bullies, when they reach adulthood, realize they've hurt others and work hard to make amends. Some apologize to their former victims, and this can be met with acceptance and forgiveness, but sometimes it isn't. Feelings of guilt and remorse can stick with former bullies for years.

into lockers, sucker punching them in the hallways, or knocking books out of their hands.

Some physical bullies start with threats. Then they might start bumping into targets "accidentally." Or they might step on the back of their shoes or steal something of importance, like a cell phone or money. Some have suggested that victims should ignore being bullied. But if the victim doesn't complain and teachers don't react, bullies often get more violent. Not all teachers and administrators are aware of or helpful about the problem, however. Some families have even had to go as far as suing school systems to get justice for their bullied children—

Some boys roughhouse a lot, but it's usually just in good fun, not bullying.

and just to get the bullies to stop.

BOYS WHO BULLY

Roughhousing, particularly between boys, is common. This is true especially between two opponents equal in size and age. In rough play, if one person wants to stop, the fight usually ends. If it is bullying, the bully probably won't stop. The attacks are imbalanced and often repeated.

There are many different ways that boys bully each other. One dangerous form of bullying is kicking other boys in the groin area.

BOYS BULLYING GIRLS

Many music videos, movies, and TV programs show men controlling women. Some boys mock any behavior they consider "girly," such as crying. They call other boys names like "sissy," "little girl," or worse. So it is not surprising that male bullies might treat girls with contempt.

Sometimes bullies will do the same kind of physical bullying to girls that they do to boys. Other times, the bullying takes a more sexual form. Some boys grope girls, snap their bra straps, rip their clothes, or otherwise humiliate them physically. Some attacks include sexual assault.

GIRLS WHO BULLY

Girls have a reputation for emotional bullying. But girls can be physical bullies, too. In 2018, the *Daily Mirror* reported an incident in Russia in which a fourteen-year-old girl was beaten severely by five girls between the ages of thirteen and fourteen. The teens filmed the entire incident. The beating lasted about three hours, and the victim ended up with a concussion and severe internal injuries.

Former bullies who can recognize their own guilt are lucky. Those students will most likely have a better outcome in life. If they can be sorry for what they did, they can change their behavior. It's the ones who are numb to the effects of their actions, or who feel they were justified, who are in danger.

According to a 2013 study at the University of Texas, Dallas, bullies are far more likely to engage in criminal behavior as adults. The study followed four hundred men over a long period to track their behavior, and almost half of those who had admitted to bullying behavior as teens went on to commit crimes. The men were also more likely to be repeat offenders.

Other research, published in the *Archives of Pediatric and Adolescent Medicine*, has suggested that bullies are more likely to grow up to abuse their spouses. According to a Harvard School

Bullies and former bullies may find a new path through the help of a therapist.

of Public Health study of more than 1,400 men between ages eighteen and thirty-five, those who remembered being school bullies were four times likelier to attack their partners than those who didn't bully. The report said, "Individuals who are likely to perpetrate abusive behaviors against others may do so across childhood into adulthood."

CAN BULLIES CHANGE?

Bullies can change. So rather than making excuses for them, many experts today believe the kindest thing adults can do for bullies is to stop them. That could mean counseling. But it could also mean giving effective consequences for their actions. When bullies punch, slap, and hurt others, they show that they do not have the appropriate social boundaries they need to develop into healthy adults. But when they are taught to act appropriately, bullies can learn to retrain their brains. They can gain self-control that will help keep them from causing harm to themselves and others in the future.

MYTHS AND FACTS ABOUT BULLYING

Myth: Girls don't engage in physical bullying.

Fact: While boys are far more likely to bully physically, girls have been reported to engage in this type of behavior as well.

Myth: Bullying is just a part of growing up.

Fact: Bullying happens frequently in adolescence, but that doesn't mean it should be an accepted part of the teen experience. If ignored, bullying can lead to poor self-esteem, struggles with anxiety, or other issues later in life.

Myth: Fighting back is the only way to stop a bully.

Fact: Being the victim of a bully can make a person feel angry or afraid. And sometimes it might seem like the best thing to do is just to defend yourself by fighting back. But this can lead to injury, or you can get in trouble for fighting and face bigger consequences in school or at home.

19

Victims and Bystanders

The novel *Let the Right One In* is about a bullied twelve-year-old boy, Oskar, who befriends a mysterious neighbor girl, Eli, with dark and terrible powers. The bullying escalates, putting Oskar in grave danger, and Eli, who it is revealed is actually a vampire, takes grisly revenge on the bullies. While this is a fantasy story, a lot of victims feel angry and have an urge to take revenge. They imagine their bullies being hurt and humiliated. But, in reality, revenge only causes more pain. Let's look at some alternatives.

Certain behaviors help reduce victims' risk. The first step is to avoid the bullies. If possible, people who are bullied should travel with friends and stay away from deserted areas. But when face to face with a bully, targets can still try to stop trouble before it starts.

The movie *Let the Right One In* offers a highly fictionalized glimpse of one boy's struggle with bullying.

The first trick is for people who are bullied to practice confident behavior. They can try standing taller. They can speak more forcefully. They can yell, "You don't have the right to act cruel," or "You may *not* talk to me—or anyone—disrespectfully!" Or targets can act bored and say, "Really," "No kidding," or "That's one opinion." Most important, victims should try to breathe deeply and keep control of their emotions as much as possible.

DEESCALATING AN ATTACK

If bullies still move to attack, targets should leave. They should walk—without turning their back on the bully—or run to a safe place. Unfortunately, it isn't always possible to avoid being physically attacked by a determined bully.

If possible, people who are bullied should not hit back. In the past, many people said to sock a bully in the jaw or show him or her who is boss. However, these days that means both parties can get into trouble. This advice also does not work if there are several bullies hurting one person. Many bullies like to fight. If their targets hit back, bullies can become even more violent.

FINDING HELP

After an attack, people who are bullied should immediately go to the school nurse to check for long-term damage, especially if there is a possible head injury, bruises, or cuts. Some students have suffered concussions, double vision, punctured eardrums,

If bullying escalates to violence and someone gets hurt, it's past time to seek help. Talk to a trusted adult, like a school guidance counselor.

broken bones, and other problems that need attention. These injuries should be documented by the nurse and separately by the victim. Then the victim should immediately report the attack to a school administrator in as calm and reasonable a voice as possible. The target of a bully can tell the administrator that he or she will be telling his or her parents and they will figure out what steps to take next. Then the bullied person should ask how the school can protect him or her from the bully in the future. Bullying victims shouldn't keep silent—they have a right to be safe.

Targets should let their parents or guardians know what's happening. It helps to bring up the subject at a quiet time, when they can explain the problem to their parents in detail. Then they can work with their parents to practice strategies on how to handle the bullying situation. Some strategies include the following:

Role-playing. Targets can practice being assertive with the help of family members (or friends) who will play the role of the bully and suggest strategies.

Put it in writing. The bullied person should keep a detailed record of dates of encounters with the bully. These encounters can include threats, physical attacks, or copies of threatening e-mails. They can include photos of bruises or cuts. If parents either call or meet with the school, they should send an e-mail confirming their understanding of what happened in the meeting and what kinds of actions will be taken next. That kind of document can prove that the family tried to resolve the issue. Documentation is important because bullies might also make charges against the target.

Targets' rights. Together, targets and their families can research their legal rights. If a school doesn't protect a target, the target and his or her guardians should keep pursuing the matter. Contact the school board or even the police. Some attacks, especially those that have a sexual or racial component, can be considered hate crimes. A complaint can be filed with the government.

In short, whatever it takes, it's worth getting justice for bullying. Not only does it help the bullied person, but it also keeps other kids from being hurt in the future. And it even

Journaling can help a victim get her feelings out on paper and provide aid on her path to recovery.

helps the bully overcome his or her harmful habits. Everyone in the school will benefit.

MOVING ON

Reclaiming their lives can help victims. Keeping a journal allows people who have been bullied to let out bad feelings—and remember positive things in their lives, too. Victims can join out-of-school activities like youth groups or drama clubs. There, they can meet new people and try out new interests. Exercise helps. Dance or martial arts classes can help a bully's victims get exercise to gain strength. It can also make them feel more confident. It may also help give targets something positive to look forward to each day until the bullying problem is solved.

WHAT IT MEANS TO BE A BYSTANDER

A bystander is one who stays in the background while others are victimized. Some bystanders could be called passive bullies. They might not start trouble, but they might taunt the target or join in the attack.

NATIONAL BULLYING PREVENTION MONTH

October is National Bullying Prevention Month, and students are finding lots of fun new ways to fight bullying in their schools. Schools hold bullying prevention dances, students plan flash mobs, drama performances, and many more. The first Monday of October is World Day of Bullying Prevention, and a great time to kick off antibullying awareness activities. Students can participate by befriending students they don't know and trying to get them involved in school activities. Students are also encouraged to help educate others on ways to avoid simply being a bystander.

Other bystanders are afraid. They don't want to be called tattletales. Some bystanders fear being physically hurt by a bully. Others think teachers won't listen to them. Still others may believe that the people being bullied deserve the treatment they get because they don't fit in.

Another reason people don't help is because of "the bystander effect." Sometimes people think that if there are a lot of witnesses to bullying, someone else will help. So if there's a crowd, each bystander may feel less responsibility. But actually, the chances that someone will help are smaller in a large crowd. In January 2011, thirteen-year-old Nadin Khoury was beaten up by seven bigger boys on the way home from school in Upper Darby, Pennsylvania. Although he was punched, kicked, stomped on his chest, dragged through snow, kicked, shoved upside down on a tree, and hung on a fence, not one bystander called 911 or tried to rescue him until a woman finally broke up the fight and drove him to safety in her vehicle.

STEPPING IN

Most bullies like an audience. And yet, according to a study reported in *Social Development* magazine, more than half the time, bullying stops within ten seconds of a bystander stepping in to help. Bystanders may not be guilty of actual bullying. But if they just stand by and watch other students be hurt by bullying, they are guilty of allowing harm to occur. They aren't innocent if they let bullying happen. So what can they do?

Bystanders can be direct. They can say firmly, "Cut it out." They can distract the bullies by saying, "A teacher's coming." They can say to the target, "Hey, Liz, come here. I need to talk to you," to get her away from the bully.

Bystanders should also get help from an adult. If necessary, they can call 911. Another thing bystanders can do is act as witnesses afterward. Sometimes no matter who started a fight, both parties get punished equally. Reporting what actually happened can keep someone from being victimized twice. The organization Bullying Bystanders Unite suggests that bystanders use their smartphones to record bullying incidents as evidence to show school officials or the police. They say that if one bully is hurting someone, go to a safe place and call 911. But if one or more bullies are physically attacking someone and there are at least four bystanders, one should call 911. The rest should hold up their phones to record the bullying episode. Even if the phones don't record, bullies may be scared of being caught and run away.

BEING A GOOD BYSTANDER

Bystanders should get angry, not only because of the effect of bullying on victims but on themselves as well. Bystanders

Speaking up when someone else is suffering is scary and difficult, but it can help put an end to the situation.

have a right not to be terrorized by seeing other students hurt. And they should not have to fear that they could be next. The guilt of being a bystander who could have done something and didn't can linger for years. On the other hand, fighting bullying can give bystanders a new sense of pride and power. There are many more bystanders than there are bullies. So bystanders can stand up against bullying.

Some bystanders have found other ways to help. In Bergen County, New Jersey, straight student Courtney La Morte is president of the Gay-Straight Alliance of her school. She wears a special rainbow bracelet, as do many members, to identify herself as a safe person to come to for people who are bullied for their sexual orientation. The Gay-Straight Alliance at her school also sponsors Days of Silence and other events to raise awareness of the difficulties that LGBTQ students face.

10 GREAT QUESTIONS

TO ASK A SCHOOL PRINCIPAL

1. If I'm being bullied, where can I go for help?

2. What is the school's policy on bullying?

3. What activities and events are being planned for National Bullying Prevention Month?

4. How can I help create a Gay-Straight Alliance at this school?

5. What should I do if I see someone being bullied?

6. What should I do if bullying has started to affect my performance at school?

7. Where can I go for support as an LGBTQ student?

8. What should I do if I'm called a racial slur?

9. What can the school do if I'm being cyberbullied?

10. Where can I go for help if I'm feeling depressed or anxious as a result of bullying?

CHAPTER FOUR

Bullying and Society

Today, students often carry and have access to electronic devices. Therefore, when a bullying incident occurs, teens can take out their phones and film. A YouTube video from Australia became an international sensation. It showed twelve-year-old Richard Gale punching a heavyset sixteen-year-old, Casey Heynes. Then Casey snapped. He picked up Richard and threw him down on the ground, hard. When people saw the video, many said that Casey was a hero for fighting the bully. But the case remained controversial. Both boys got suspended. It turns out that Casey was a frequent target at the school. But is it really fair for a tenth grader to slam a seventh grader to the ground? Casey could have caused serious

Is fighting back against a bully an act of self-defense or simply adding to the violence?

damage to the smaller, younger boy. Then he would face legal consequences. What is clear is that by allowing bullying to continue, the school had a mess on its hands.

People used to think bullying that could never be stopped. In the bad old days, and sometimes even today, schools would tell victims to stand up for themselves—even when a single victim was faced with a mob of attackers.

But not everything schools have tried has been successful. For instance, counseling victims to be nice to bullies or go along with their taunts can just incite the bullies to be crueler. It also undermines the dignity of the person who is bullied. In other schools, targets have been asked to forgive bullies' cruelty because the bullies must feel bad about themselves to act so badly. That puts bullies' victims in an unfair position by placing their attackers' needs above their own.

Another strategy that schools have tried was putting bullies and their targets together to solve their problems. Targets were encouraged to explain how hurt they felt by the bullying. This method is controversial, as victims might feel forced them to relive a traumatic experience. Meanwhile the bully might get to enjoy the memory of the cruelty he or she inflicted.

Another problem is that many students—both victims and bystanders—have felt reluctant to approach teachers because they feel they won't be believed or helped.

Several studies show that there is a wide gap between teachers' perceptions of their effectiveness and students' views. Some situations are also unclear, and there are teachers who like to take a "let them work it out for themselves" approach.

But even if it is hard for teachers and school administrators, assuring student safety is still their responsibility under the law.

In the 1970s, Professor Dan Olweus at the University of Bergen, Norway, challenged the idea that bullying is normal. Instead of considering bullying to be an individual problem, he proposed that bullying is a system in which school administrators, bystanders, and others have a large role to play. He wrote a book titled *Aggression in the Schools: Bullies and Whipping Boys*, talking about his ideas. Then Olweus tried different techniques that showed bullying can be stopped. In the 1980s, he conducted the first systematic intervention study against bullying in the world.

Since then, most states in the United States have passed laws that require schools to have antibullying policies. Many of them are based on Olweus's original plan. They focus on the ideas that every person in a school—bully, bystander, target, cafeteria worker, teacher, and administrator—has a responsibility to help stop bullying and that the problem is not that the victim deserves to be hurt, but that the bully is acting in an antisocial way. It encourages bystanders to become justice seekers and to help and support the victim.

Some features of successful antibullying programs include the following:

- Asking students to map out dangerous areas in the school. When students identify unsafe areas, such as stairwells, bathrooms, and locker rooms, staff members can be assigned to monitor these problem locations.

- Giving counseling and support to bullies' victims to help them regain confidence.
- Teaching bystanders how to be more assertive.
- Giving consequences and counseling to bullies to teach them not to bully.
- Having a system for students to be able to report bullying anonymously, such as a bully box or confidential website.
- Training adults at the school, such as bus drivers and teachers, to know how to respond to bullying, including reporting incidents for the administration to act on.
- Putting the school in charge of the students' safety.

For these programs to be successful, the adults who run a school and the parents of students who go there must recognize that children deserve the same sense of safety that they expect for themselves. And they have to be serious about getting that result.

IT GETS BETTER

After several gay teens died by suicide, a national columnist named Dan Savage started a YouTube project called It Gets Better. His point was to tell bullied kids, especially gay ones, to hang on because adult life can be so much better. But the message works for everyone.

Even though being bullied can be very harmful, there are lessons people can learn from hard times. Being bullied can turn people into justice seekers. They may become more tolerant. And they may find an inner strength (and a sense of self) that they never knew they had.

American society is doing more, too. The problem of bullying is getting more and more attention. On March 10, 2011, President Barack Obama led the first ever antibullying summit at the White House. Now, some famous people, such as actress Blake Lively, are starting to share their bullying experiences. According to *People* magazine, she said, "Kids used to make fun of me in elementary school by calling me Big Bird (because I was 'too tall' and had 'yellow' hair)." Actress Emily Blunt was picked on for her childhood stutter. Spider-

It Gets Better project founder Dan Savage celebrates National Coming Out Day in 2012.

Man actor Tom Holland, who once starred in *Billy Eliot, the Musical,* was bullied for enjoying dancing. "You couldn't hit me hard enough to stop me from doing it," he added, though. Many celebrities want young people to know that most kids survive the humiliation and pain of bullying and go on to lead rich, productive lives.

First Lady Melania Trump reminds young people to Be Best at an event in 2018.

First Lady Melania Trump started the "Be Best" initiative in 2018, with a goal of raising awareness about cyberbullying. "I will also work to shine a spotlight on the people, organizations and programs across the country that are helping children overcome the many issues they are facing as they grow up," said Trump during her address at the launch of the initiative.

CUTTING BULLYING DOWN TO SIZE

Many young people are fighting bullying by joining—and creating—antibullying programs. They are taking the cause of fighting bullying into their own hands.

Singer Lady Gaga was once stuffed into a garbage can in middle school by a bully. Now she is an antibullying activist and has showed support for younger antibullying activists, including Emily-Anne Rigal. A former target, Rigal started an antibullying web page and Facebook site called WeStopHate.org. She started the site after she was bullied herself. According to her website, WeStopHate "is more than just an anti-bullying program...It's a call to action to stop hate: stop hating on yourself, stop hating on others, stop letting others hate on you. Unlike most programs, there is two-way communication: we

A SAFE SCHOOL ENVIRONMENT FOR LGBTQ TEENS

Being LGBTQ in school can be a minefield for a lot of students. A 2017 report by the Centers for Disease Control and Prevention says that 33 percent of LGBTQ students have reported being bullied on school grounds.

Help protect LGBTQ students by being an ally in the following ways:

Protect their privacy: If a friend or fellow student confides in you that he or she has a certain gender or sexual identity, keep that information to yourself, even if you suspect other people already know and don't see the harm in confirming their suspicions. This goes for the individual's family members and close friends, too! Outing someone is rude, but it can also be potentially dangerous for the student in question.

Offer acceptance: Even if your religious beliefs might lead you to condemn LGBTQ people, you owe it to your fellow students to be accepting and treat everyone equally. Your own beliefs should not be imposed on others unless they ask for your input.

Engage with kindness: LGBTQ teens often feel rejected, depressed, or afraid. If you're an ally, express yourself through your kindness. Report any abuse you see online and in person. Get involved with in-school LGBTQ alliance programs.

continually remind each other that stopping hate isn't something to do once, but it's a practice and approach to live by each day."

Young people like Emily-Anne Rigal are taking matters into their own hands. The next generation of teens has the chance to make sure that life gets better—not just when they're adults—but starting today while they're still in school. But fixing the serious problem that is physical bullying is not just the responsibility of kids. It can't be solved unless it involves families, the schools, and the larger community. Only a universal understanding and commitment to fixing the issue with help bring an end to bullying and bullying behaviors.

GLOSSARY

ACTIVIST A person who works for a cause.

AGGRESSION Hostility or anger.

ASSAULT To attack.

AUTISM A spectrum disorder (one with a wide variety of linked conditions) characterized by a struggle with social skills, behaviors, and/or communication.

BULLY A person who uses aggressive behavior repeatedly to hurt or frighten a target.

BYSTANDER An onlooker.

CONTEMPT A feeling of extreme disrespect for something or someone.

COUNSELING Professional assistance in resolving a personal, social, or psychological issue.

CYBERBULLYING Intimidating or hurting someone else by using the internet to spread rumors or say cruel things.

EPILEPSY A neurological disorder characterized by abnormal brain activity that results in seizures, unusual behavior, or loss of awareness.

GROPE To grab part of someone else's body without his or her permission.

INTERVENTION Taking action to stop a course of events.

REVENGE An action taken in retaliation for harm or an injustice.

RUMOR A circulating story that may or may not be true and is sometimes passed around to damage another person's reputation.

SCHEMA An underlying pattern of thinking.

SELF-ESTEEM Self-respect.

SUBMISSIVENESS Weak, resigned, or passive behavior.

TARGET The victim of a bully.

VERBAL ABUSE A type of abuse wherein words, insults, criticism, or other verbal means are used to cause harm to another person.

VULNERABLE Being an easy target for physical or emotional attack or harm.

FOR MORE INFORMATION

BullyingCanada
27009-471 Smythe Street
Fredericton, NB E3B 9M1
Canada
(877) 352-4497
Website: http://www.bullyingcanada.ca
Facebook and Twitter: @BullyingCanada

Bullying Canada's website encourages people to "Be the change you want to see. Make bullying stop." Young people who are experiencing bullying troubles can call the number above.

GLSEN National Headquarters
110 William Street, 30th Floor
New York, NY 10038
(212) 727-0135
Website: https://www.glsen.org
Facebook and Twitter: @GLSEN
Instagram: @glsen

The Gay, Lesbian and Straight Education Network (GLSEN) helps schools provide antibullying programs. It also offers useful information to students, including how to file complaints for bullied young people.

National Bullying Prevention Center
PACER Center, Inc.
8161 Normandale Boulevard

Bloomington, MN 55437
(800) 537-2237
Website: http://www.pacer.org
Facebook: @PACERsNationalBullyingPreventionCenter
Instagram: @pacer_nbpc
Twitter: @PACER_NBPC

The National Bullying Prevention Center provides resources for young people and adults to help fight bullying in schools. It also provides resources focused on the bullying of children with disabilities.

Safe & Humane Schools
Clemson University, YFCS
321 Brackett Hall
Clemson, SC 29634
(864) 656-6712
Website: https://olweus.sites.clemson.edu
Facebook: @olweus
Twitter: @OBPPClemson

The Olweus Program's goals are to reduce and prevent bullying problems among schoolchildren and improve peer relations at schools.

StopBullying.gov
US Department of Health and Human Services
200 Independence Avenue SW
Washington, DC 20201
(877) 696-6775
Website: http://www.hhs.gov

Facebook: @StopBullying.gov
Instagram: @stopbullyinggov
Twitter: @StopBullyingGov

The website provides age-appropriate materials for young people, parents, and teachers on how to understand and stop bullying. It is managed by the Department of Health and Human Services in partnership with the Department of Education and Department of Justice.

The Trevor Project
PO Box 69232
West Hollywood, CA 90069
(310) 271-8845
Website: https://www.thetrevorproject.org
Facebook: @TheTrevorProject
Instagram: @trevorproject
Twitter: @TrevorProject

The Trevor Project is a website and a hotline for gay and questioning youth. In addition, students who need help can get advice from the site or can call the Trevor Lifeline.

FOR FURTHER READING

Dawson, Juno. *This Book Is Gay*. Naperville, IL: Sourcebooks, 2015.

Dunham, Kelli. *The Girl's Body Book*. 4th ed. Kennebunkport, ME: Applesauce, 2017.

50 Cent. *Playground: The Mostly True Story of a Former Bully*. New York, NY: Razorbill, 2011.

Halloran, Janine. *Coping Skills for Kids Workbook: Over 75 Coping Strategies to Help Kids Deal with Stress, Anxiety and Anger*. Eau Claire, WI: PESI Publshing & Media, 2018.

Hemmen, Lucie. *The Teen Girl's Survival Guide: Ten Tips for Making Friends, Avoiding Drama, and Coping with Social Stress*. Oakland, CA: Instant Help, 2015.

Jennings, Jazz. *Being Jazz: My Life as a (Transgender) Teen*. Toronto, ON: Ember, 2017.

Mardell, Ashley. *The ABC's of LGBT+*. Coral Gables, FL: Mango, 2016.

Mayrock, Aija. *The Survival Guide to Bullying: Written by a Teen*. New York, NY: Scholastic, 2015.

Meeks, Lisa, and Tracy Loye Masterson. *Parties, Dorms and Social Norms: A Crash Course in Safe Living for Young Adults on the Autism Spectrum*. London, UK: Jessica Kingsley, 2016.

Morgan, Nicola. *Positively Teen: A Practical Guide to a More Positive, More Confident You*. New York, NY: Poppy, 2019.

Raja, Sheela, and Jaya Raja Ashrafi. *The PTSD Survival Guide for Teens: Strategies to Overcome Trauma, Build Resilience, and Take Back Your Life*. Oakland, CA: Instant Help, 2018.

BIBLIOGRAPHY

Aleccia, JoNel. "Peanut Menace? Bullies Use Food to Torment Allergic Kids." MSNBC, November 22, 2010. http://www .nbcnews.com/id/39389689/ns/health-childrens_health/t /peanut-menace-bullies-use-food-torment-allergic-kids/# .XJAVgaeZOqA.

Brown, Eryn. "Study Links Teenage Bullying to Social Status." *Los Angeles Times*, February 7, 2011. http://articles.latimes .com/2011/feb/07/health/la-he-mean-girls-20110208.

Burke, Dave. "Savage Bullies Stamped on Girl, 14, So Hard She May Have Been Left Infertile." *Daily Mirror*, November 13, 2018. https://www.mirror.co.uk/news/world-news/savage -bullies-stamped-girl-14-13581984.

Coloroso, Barbara. "Bully, Bullied, Bystander…and Beyond." Teaching Tolerance: A Project of the Southern Poverty Law Center, Spring 2011. https://www.tolerance.org/magazine /spring-2011/bully-bullied-bystanderand-beyond.

Darley, J. M., and B. Latané. "Bystander Intervention in Emergencies: Diffusion of Responsibility." *Journal of Personality and Social Psychology*, 1968. Vol. 8, pp. 377–383.

Farley, Melissa. "What's Up with the Bullied Boy in That Video?" *USA Today*, May 15, 2018. https://www.usatoday.com/story /life/allthemoms/news/2018/05/15/standwithkeaton-bullied -boy-viral-video/34920963.

Golijan, Rosa. "Emotional Interview Reveals Why Boy Bodyslammed Bully." Today, March 21, 2011. https://www .today.com/money/emotional-interview-reveals-why-boy -bodyslammed-bully-1C8368682.

Green, Alison. "I Didn't Get a Job Because I Was a Bully in High School." Ask a Manager, April 25, 2017. https://www .askamanager.org/2017/04/i-didnt-get-a-job-because-i-was-a -bully-in-high-school.html.

It Gets Better Project. "What Is the It Gets Better Project." Retrieved March 11, 2019. http://www.itgetsbetter.org/pages /about-it-gets-better-project.

Juvonen, Jaana. "I Study the Psychology of Adolescent Bullies. Trump Makes Perfect Sense to Me." *Washington Post*, May 23, 2017. https://www.washingtonpost.com/posteverything /wp/2017/05/23/i-study-the-psychology-of-adolescent-bullies -trump-makes-perfect-sense-to-me/?utm _term=.8eb968161e7f.

Juvonen, J., and E. F. Gross. "The Rejected and the Bullied: Lessons About Social Misfits from Developmental Psychology." In K. D. Williams, J. P. Forgas, and W. von Hippel (eds). *The Social Outcast: Ostracism, Social Exclusion, Rejection, and Bullying* (pp. 155–170). New York, NY: Psychology Press, 2005.

Law, Jacob. "Not a Story about a Bullying Victim Not a Story about a Bullying Advocate Just a Story about Me." Teens Against Bullying, March 7, 2019. https:// pacerteensagainstbullying.org/advocacy-for-others/real-teens -speak-out.

Olweus Bullying Prevention Program. Clemson University: Institute on Family & Neighborhood Life. Retrieved March 4, 2019. http://www.clemson.edu/olweus/history.htm.

Pacer Center's Kids Against Bullying. "What Is Bullying?" Retrieved March 18, 2019. https://www .pacerkidsagainstbullying.org/what-is-bullying.

Pacer's National Bullying Prevention Center. "Bullying and Harassment of Students with Disabilities." Retrieved March 18, 2019. https://www.pacer.org/bullying/resources/students-with -disabilities.

Pincus, Debbie, MS. "Child and Teen Bullying: How to Help When Your Kid Is Bullied." EmpoweringParents. Retrieved

March 18, 2019. https://www.empoweringparents.com/article
/child-and-teen-bullying-how-to-help-when-your-kid-is
-bullied.

StopBullying.gov. "Facts About Bullying." Retrieved March 18,
2019. https://www.stopbullying.gov/media/facts/index.html.

Yagoda, Maria. "Lady Gaga, Bella Hadid, Priyanka Chopra &
More Stars Who've Open Up About the Bullying They Faced
as Kids." *People*, October 9, 2018. https://people.com
/celebrity/bullying-rumer-willis-jessica-alba-jessica-simpson
-and-eva-mendes/#tom-holland.

INDEX

ABOUT THE AUTHORS

Pam T. Glaser faced her own bullies growing up. She decided that writing about bullying would help her better understand her bullies and her own experiences. She writes frequently about issues for teens and lives in Omaha, Nebraska.

Like many young people, Alexandra Hanson-Harding was physically bullied in elementary school and junior high. Books inspired her during those tough times, so when she grew up, she wanted to write for young people. She is the author of many books and articles, but she finds it especially meaningful to write for children and teens who struggle with the issue of bullying.

PHOTO CREDITS

Cover Tomas Rodriguez/Corbis/Getty Images; p. 4 Todd Williamson/Getty Images; p. 7 Sean Justice/Photonica/Getty Images; p. 9 selinofoto/Shutterstock.com; p. 11 tommaso79/Shutterstock.com; p. 12 Jun Sato/TAS18/Getty Images; pp. 14, 18, 27 Monkey Business Images/Shutterstock.com; p. 16 Fuse/Corbis/Getty Images; p. 20 Allstar Picture Library/Alamy Stock Photo; p. 22 Rawpixel.com/Shutterstock.com; p. 24 cglade/iStock/Getty Images; p. 29 golubovystock/Shutterstock.com; p. 33 Cindy Ord/Getty Images; p. 34 Bloomberg/Getty Images; cover and interior graphic elements Olgastocker/Shutterstock.com (diagonal pattern), Solomnikov/Shutterstock.com (splatters).

Design & Layout: Brian Garvey; Editor: Bethany Bryan; Photo Researcher: Sherri Jackson